Memory of a
Large Christmas

Memory of a Large Christmas

by LILLIAN SMITH

Decorations by CONSTANCE McMILLAN

W · W · NORTON & COMPANY

New York · London

Copyright © 1961, 1962 by Lillian Smith

Published simultaneously in Canada by George J. McLeod Limited, Toronto.

Printed in the United States of America

First published as a Norton paperback 1980.

Library of Congress Cataloging in Publication Data
Smith, Lillian Eugenia, 1897–1966.
  Memory of a large Christmas.
  (A Norton paperback)
  1. Smith, Lillian Eugenia, 1897–1966—Biography—
Youth. 2. Authors, American—20th century—
Biography. 3. Christmas. I. Title.
PS3537.M653Z47   1980   813'.52   80–20851

ISBN 0–393–00038–9

W. W. Norton & Company, Inc. 500 Fifth Avenue, New York, N.Y. 10110
W. W. Norton & Company Ltd. 25 New Street Square, London EC4A 3NT

1 2 3 4 5 6 7 8 9 0

To Esther,

who collaborated as little sister

in all my young dreams

Contents

Memory of a Large Christmas   9
Christmas Kitchen Fifty Years Ago   65

ℛ＊ℛ＊ℛ＊ℛ＊ℛ＊ℛ＊ℛ＊ℛ＊ℛ

Memory of a
Large Christmas

ℛ＊ℛ＊ℛ＊ℛ＊ℛ＊ℛ＊ℛ＊ℛ＊ℛ

Everything about our family was big: there were nine of us and our mother and father and a cousin or two, and Little Grandma when it was her turn to stay with us, and Big Grandma when it was hers, and there were three bird dogs and four cats and their kittens and once a small alligator and a pet coon. And the house took them all in. And still there were empty corners and stairways and pantries, and maybe the winter parlor would have nobody in it, but if it did you could go to the summer parlor, or if you felt too crowded you could slip in the closet under the stairs and crawl on and on until it grew small and low, then you could get down on your stomach and crawl way back where things were quiet and dim, and sometimes you liked that.

But not often. Most of the time you wanted to be with the others racing round the veranda, or huddled up somewhere playing games. It was only when Big Grandma came that we began to scramble for hide-outs, for Big Grandma filled up the whole place. She could scrouge even Christmas.

We dreaded her coming. We'd moan, Oh Mama why! And our mother would look at us, her dark eyes growing darker, darker, then she'd say softly, "Your grandmother is very good with the hog killing."

My big brothers, two, three, four of them would launch a collective protest: old Japers and Desto from the farm could handle the hogs. And Papa was there. Why Big Grandma! She gets in the way, showing the men how hogs should be stuck, calling them to do this and that, and all the time hogs squealing and Grandma getting too close to the knives and the wind blowing smoke every which-away from fires under pots where water is heating for the scraping, oh Mama!

Mother soothed her rebellious sons, "Remember the sausage. Nobody can make sausage as good as your grandmother's; she knows just how to dry the sage and rub and crumble it just right and how much red pepper to put in and she never puts in too much fat." Mother was expert in the fine usages of reiteration, "And she stuffs the skins just right," turning to the Twelve Year Old—"last year you helped her and you loved it."

"I didn't have no sense last year. I was just a kid."

Mother's voice begged. "You love her sausage and hot biscuits, everyone of you—"

"But Mama—"

"You love her sausage, remember."

Yes, we did. But we didn't love Big Grandma. Especially at Christmas.

Christmas began when pecans started falling. The early November rains loosened the nuts from their outer shells and sent them plopping like machine gun bullets on the roof of the veranda. In the night, you'd listen and you'd know IT would soon be here.

IT was *not* Thanksgiving. We skipped that day. At school, there were exercises, yes, and we dressed up like New England Pilgrims and play-acted Priscilla and Miles Standish and made like we had just landed on Plymouth Rock. But the truth is, the only Plymouth Rocks we saw in our minds were the black and white hens scratching round at the hen house. In those days, the Pilgrims and Thanksgiving did not dent the imaginations of little Southerners, some of whose parents wouldn't concede they had a thing to be thankful for, anyway. It was football that elevated the day into a festival—but that was later than these memories.

We eased over the national holiday without one tummy ache. Turkey? that was Christmas. Pumpkin pie? not for us. Sweet potato pie was Deep South dessert in the fall. We had it once or twice a week. Now and then, Mother varied it with sweet potato pone—rather nice if you don't try it often: raw sweet potato was grated, mixed with cane syrup, milk, eggs and spices and slowly baked, then served with thick unbeaten cream; plain, earthy, caloric and good. But not Christmasy.

Pecans were. Everybody in town had at least one tree. Some had a dozen. No matter. Pecans were prestige. They fitted Christmas.

And so you lay there, listening to the drip drip of rain and plop plop of nuts, feeling something good is going to happen, something good and it won't be long now. And you'd better sneak out early in the morning before your five brothers and three sisters and get you a few pecans and hide them. Strange how those nuts made squirrels out of us. Nothing was more plentiful and yet we hid piles of them all over the place. Of course, when there are nine of you and the cousins, you get in the habit of hiding things.

Our father chose the auspicious Monday to shake the trees. (Our weekly school holiday was Monday.) The shaking occurred after breakfast. He would stay long enough from the mill to get us well organized. You organized nine kids and the cousins when Big Grandma was around; if you didn't, she would take over—and there'd be a riot.

I cannot remember a nonconforming breakfast on tree-shaking day, but on ordinary days breakfast could be highly unpredictable. One never knew where rebellion would break out.

Our father customarily arose at five o'clock, drank a cup of coffee, walked to the mill, got things going there; got the logging train off to the woods, the mules off to the turpentine farm, got things going at the planing mill, the dry kiln, the shingle mill and the big mill, got things going at the commissary, going at the office, going at the ice plant, going at the Supply Store which he owned half interest in, and at the light plant and water works which he owned three-quarters interest in. Then, with everything going, he walked home to have breakfast with his children.

We were all in the dining room when he came back. A fire was sputtering in the fireplace if the day was cold, the bay window was fluttering with windy white curtains and sunshine and the nervous cage of the canary who was being stalked by one of the cats. The big long table was spread with a white Irish damask cloth—one of Mother's few self-indulgences. There were platters at each end of mullet roe (crisply fried), or perhaps, smothered steak; there were three bowls of grits, and four plates of thin light biscuits and two dishes of homemade butter and three pitchers of cane syrup scattered in between.

We each had our place. The two oldest sat on either side of our mother; the two youngest sat in high chairs on either side of our father; the others sat according to age in between. You took your turn sitting by Big Granny. You sat under duress, for not only was she wide, she had a habit of reaching over to your plate with her fork when both your hands were busy and spearing the morsel you had saved for last. On the walnut-paneled wall, behind the picture (lambs huddling in terrible snow storm) was a small shelf on which lay the Bible and a thin peach-sprout switch. The Bible was read every morning. The thin switch was used to quell whatever disorder was popping up among the younger ones.

We sat down. Our father read briefly from the Bible, closed it, rested his hand on it for a moment as though it gave him strength (and I think it did) then put it back on the shelf. He returned to the table, looked round at his nine, smiled, studied a face now and then as though it was new, beamed at mother, then encouragingly asked for our verses. Each of us then said what we had gleaned from the Bible. The youngest always said, *Jesus wept*. The next one always said, *God is love*. The others were on their own. Verses began with the oldest and came down like a babbling stream to the youngest.

It was usually routine. But there were sudden uprisings. One morning, the six-year-old when his turn came, calmly shouted "Jesus wept!" Silence. A scream from the youngest, "He tant have Thesus wept, he tant it's mine he tant he tant—" A scream from the four-year-old, "He tant have my Dod is love neider he tant he tant he tant—"

"Sssh . . . nobody's going to take your Jesus wept or your G—" He turned to the deviationist. "Why, son," he asked gravely, "did you say your little sister's verse?"

"I'm tired," said son. Father looked at Mother. Mother looked at the tired one who flashed his softest smile on her. When Father was not present it worked. No response now. He looked at Big Granny who could be fetched by it, too, but B. G. had seized the opportunity to spear a big piece of roe from an unguarded plate. Six-year-old swallowed hard, "I'm plumb wore out," he quavered.

Dissent more often came from the higher echelons. There was the summer when Age Fifteen decided it was time for subversion. He came close to bringing off a successful *coup* by the simple and highly effective device of teaching the *Song of Solomon* to one and all, even the littlest. He trained with cruel disregard of all the things we wanted to dream about or run and do. His sense of timing was superb; his dominance over us was complete, for we adored Age Fifteen whose imagination never went to sleep,

we would have loved to move into his mythic mind and live there forever with him. So we chanted our lines, as he ordered, and rechanted—quick, quick, he'd say, no wait, be ready, hook on now; and finally, we were zipping along like a chain reaction and he announced we were ready.

The morning came. He led off with "How beautiful are thy feet with shoes, O prince's daughter . . . thy navel is like a round goblet which wanteth not liquor . . . thy two breasts are like two young roes that are twins . . . thy neck . . ." Each picked up his split-second cue and carried on, and it was climaxed by the two-year-old who piped out gaily, "Tay me wif flagons, tomfort me wif apples for I am thick of love."

And there was the time when one of the sisters—eleven years old that year—craving economy of effort and a smidge of excitement, specialized in the Begats. Each morning this pigtailed plump daughter sang out to the dining room her story of begetting: "Enos lived ninety years and begat Cainan . . . And Cainan lived seventy years and begat Mahalaleel . . . and Mahalaleel lived sixty-five years and begat Jared"—etc.

The parents could play it cool when they wanted to. For three mornings, they quietly ignored the giggles of the eight and the cousins, as Eleven Year Old begatted. But Eleven was too proud of her memory and her acrobatic skill with Semitic names and she loved the spotlight. The next morning she hung on to Genesis and begat and begat and begat. Her audience was hysterical. Then the two youngest, giggling wildly about what they could not comprehend, seized the chance to steal a biscuit before the Blessing and promptly choked on their dual pleasures and our father, beating alternately on two little wheezy backs, yelled (a measure reserved for near-disaster) Stop it, you!

Age Eleven, a thinskinned if loquacious show-off, blushed and began to cry silently. And Big Granny who had been having a ball spearing food off the platters along with the littlest ones put a sausage on the conquered one's plate and told her to hush and eat, eating would make anything all right and WHAT DID THE POOR CHILD DO THAT WAS SO WRONG she shouted from *her* soapbox, seizing this chance to heckle her son-in-law.

Our father looked at Mother. And Mother swiftly said,

"Papa, please say the Blessing—the other verses can wait until tomorrow."

But on tree-shaking day we were meek. We said proper verses, we bowed our heads for the Blessing, we ate quickly, did not kick each other or yap at Big Grandma.

The moment we were excused from the table we ran to the linen closet for old sheets and spread them under the trees as our father directed. We got the baskets without being told. We were gloriously good. Even the little ones listened when Papa told them not to cry if the nuts hit their heads—anyway, they didn't need to get under the tree, did they? Of course, they needed to get under the tree but they said yessuh and waved him goodby as he walked down the tiled walk which led to the street which led to his office.

The one chosen to shake the tree first was usually the eldest. But now and then, an ambitious underling snatched the honor away by bringing in wood for all twelve fireplaces without being told to or washing and polishing Mother's brougham and offering to drive her out to Cousin Lizzie's; or maybe, he cleaned (with his sisters' help) all twenty-two lamp chimneys. (The town's young electric light plant was still pretty unstable; one never knew what to count on; but my father took care of that, too, by arranging a signal of two quick blinks and one delayed one, which was the communal code for *light your oil lamps quick!* Even on its placid evenings, the light plant turned "the juice" off at nine-thirty.)

Whoever won by fair or foul means the title of shaker of the tree did a pull-up to the first limb, hefted himself to the next, skittered into the branches and began to shake. Thousands of nuts fell until sheets were covered and thickening. Everybody was picking up and filling the baskets, except the little ones who ran round and round, holding their hands up to catch the raining nuts, yelping when hit, dashing to safety, rolling over the big boys' bird dogs, racing back. The inevitable moment came when the smallest

girl whined "I gotta peepee I gotta—" But nobody was going to take her to what Mother called the Garden House, nobody was in that kind of sacrificial mood. When the piteous cries could no longer be ignored, one of the older boys sang out, My gosh, don't you know how? And shamed and desperate, she crept behind a bush as she had seen our retriever do. Soon she was back, holding up her damp hands to catch the falling nuts, begging the shaker to shake her some and everybody was begging for more nuts on his side of the tree, for his turn shaking, for another basket—

This was how Christmas began for us. Soon, the nuts had been stored in old pillow cases. Our neighbors used croker sacks, I don't know why we preferred old pillow

cases. After a few days of what our mother called "seasoning" the picking out of the nut meats took place. This was Little Granny's job, if it was her turn to be with us. We'd gather in her room and sit close to the hearth listening to her soft easy stories of panthers in the Big Swamp when she was young, how she shot one between the eyes in 1824, and of the war with the Seminoles; and every now and then, she put a broken piece of nut in our mouths; and we loved her and her stories. But when Big Granny was there, she shooed us away, ensconced herself in a rocker in a sunny place on the circular veranda, and as she rocked and sang *Bringing in the Sheaves,* she carefully cracked the nuts (she was good at it) and got them out whole; and she'd put three halves in the fruit jar and plop one in her mouth for the road, but finally quarts and quarts of pecan halves were ready for the fruit cake, and the date and pecan cake, and the Waldorf salad and the chicken salad and the chewy syrup candy you make from cane syrup with lots of homemade butter and lots of nuts—the kind you put on the back veranda for the cold air to harden while watchers take turns shooing the hen away and the bird dogs away and the cat—

Christmas was coming nearer. It was December. A cold frosty week was upon us and our father said it was fine for hog-killing. This, too, was on Monday. We were all present. The hogs were brought in from the farm, two black wash pots were brought from Aunt Chloe's back-yard where she lived in our backyard; and an awful Thing which the Fifteen-Year-Old—specializing in the French Revolution at the moment—called the "guillotine." The word made the blood flow in imaginations where already enough was flowing to streak the day with horror. The guillotine was a two-by-six plank nailed to two strong posts which were firmly embedded in the ground. There was a pulley-and-chain attached. It served as a rack from which to hang the hogs while they were being cleaned.

But first they were dipped in boiling water and scraped—
a witchbrewed process which turned black hogs to white
hogs, stunning the young spectators—then, after the scraping, the gambrel stick was fastened to the tendons of each
leg and the hogs were hoisted up to the rack and split open
and entrails and heart and liver and lights tumbled into big
tubs on the ground beneath them.

There are lacunae in my memory. I felt a profound
ambivalence about this day. I longed for it and dreaded it

like death. To us all it was orgy and holocaust, wild pleasure and terror that pounded the heart and dilated the pupils
of eyes. But even so, on the perimeter somewhere beyond
words but *there*, were visions of platters of sausage and
crisp spareribs and backbone and rice and liver-'n'-lights
stew and and . . .

So we awoke at dawn. We dressed and went out to watch the men build the fire and heat the water in the big black pots. We never took our eyes from them but crept closer, closer to the massive preparations for these primitive rites. And then, the moment came when Desto and Japers threw a squealing hog to the ground and stuck it in the throat and then lifted three or four hundred pounds of mortally wounded but still struggling flesh into the steaming barrel. By this time the youngest was running his legs off to get to Grandma's room—any grandma would do now. But the others, in a state either of paralysis or hypnosis, stayed on. And in the sudden hush came the moment when the blood began to spurt. And now, the Seven-Year-Old and her younger sister were scampering to the parlor where if you hid behind the piano you couldn't hear a sound. Two tense faces peered out now and then, but bodies were reluctant to follow; and it was only when the more curious crept to the back porch to see what was happening that she saw the big steel knife raised to slit the hog's belly. She shot through the door to the parlor and crouched behind the piano, whitefaced and tightlipped. The less daring whispered, What did you see? what did you see? But you could only shake your head.

Squatting there, behind the upright piano whose back was painted gold and stamped with the letters *Kranich & Bach*, smelling the musty dark carpet and looking at the carved walnut and damask furniture and the blue Victorian glass vases, you somehow pushed out the terror, the sense of unlimited violence. Your sister whispered, "Let's play dolls." But to play dolls on this day! No. You buried your face against the cold frame of the piano and waited waited

waited until silence came from the outside where death and
blood and squeals and glistening steel blades and smoke had
driven tranquillity off the face of the earth.

Then you crept out. You had to know what was happening in the vast silence. So you eased through the wide
hall, eased to the back porch, and down the steps—.

Nothing was happening. It was like a dream: it was
over. Nothing was hanging there. Nothing was squealing.
No anything was anywhere. The big wooden table was
clean and bare of all but the white enameled dish pans and
stew pots where Mama and the women seemed to be washing up things. And you saw that Mama's autumn rosebushes
were blooming just as they had yesterday. The pump was
dripping as it had done all your life. The big washpots were
gone. Nothing left but smoldering ashes. You walked
closer. Something strange and magic had occurred: death
had been transmuted into Food For The Family. You saw
that Desto and Japers were stacking ordinary hams and
bacon meat, and shoulders and backbone, in neat piles and
sprinkling a little salt over them. And there were your
brothers, blowing the bladders into wonderful balloons
and suddenly you were yelling, Let me let me let me its
my turn. . . . Now, the youngest was creeping out, and
Age Thirteen who had hidden upstairs in the library with
a book sauntered out with cool nonchalance as though unaware anything extraordinary had been going on. . . . And
now, in an instant, ALL THE WORLD turned into a
Good Place with a Good Father and a Good Mother and
a Good Granny who made good sausage, and a Good
Japers who said, Little Sister, come here, Old Japers will
show you how to cut a pork chop.

You went to him: and the big black hand covered the small white hand, and holding firmly to the long steel knife, the two together pressed down down on something, then Japers whispered, Hold tight! and you did, and he lifted your hand and his and the knife and came down hard—and lo, the two of you had cut a pork chop. And he was saying softly, I sho do like pork chops, don't you, Little Sister? and you whispered back, I sho do, Japers. And the two words had changed the whole world.

Tension eased from faces and pupils of eyes lost dilation and suddenly everybody went wild with confidence, wild with atavistic triumph, for once again, Man—black man and white man together—had won a victory over the animal world. And now, the kids were yelling, Let me grind its my turn, let me let me let me, and they'd grind a few times and then sneezing from the sage and pepper they'd abandon Big Granny and the sausage and run round the dim cavernous smokehouse, peering in the bins where salt meat from last year still lay, and looking at dark brown greenish moldish hams hanging from the rafters where they had cured in the smoke last winter, sniffing the salt-hickory-sugar-phosphorus of old ashes, traces of which were there from last year and the year before and the year before and the year—dashing out, now to the yard where a setting sun threw shafts of light across dark pecan trees, turning the women's faces a warm mahogany and yellowing the white pans. Racing now to the woodhouse for kindling, glad to help tote in wood for the twelve fireplaces tonight, glad to be a part of the big human family, glad to belong to the house where you were born.

Big and endless, that house. I am sure that were I to see it now, it would seem shrunken in size, for all these years it has been growing in my memory and, too, I had only a small world to measure it by when I was a child.

Our mother and father started their marriage in bleak disordered Reconstruction days with almost no money at all. They began in a two-room house set in the middle of

a town block on College Street. As each child came along my father added a room, and the year in between—for we arrived regularly like steps—if he had lucked out with his business ventures he'd add something extra: a winter parlor one year; a summer parlor; and when waterworks came to our town he added four bathrooms; and one prosperous year he built a fifteen-foot veranda round the whole house, except the wing where the dining room and kitchen were. There were deep mysterious closets in almost every room and some of them had small doors at the rear through which you could crawl in the dark edging one shoulder through, then the other—and suddenly there you'd be: on the ground under the house among great squatting brick pillars which held the big house on their backs. In the dim eerie light you'd see, maybe, a toadfrog close to your hand

blinking at you, and you'd feel it didn't think you belonged here, and sometimes, just as you were sliding through the narrow hole you were sure the big squatting pillars were saying things but they never spoke while you were there. A winding halfdark stairway led to the second floor from the wide hall which in itself was a room with fireplace and mantel and pictures on the walls and a black tufted leather couch. And there was a stairway on the back

You went round saying boldly, There's a beautiful doll in Mr. Pennington's store only it hasn't any clothes on, but it would look beautiful in a hemstitched white polka-dotted dress with little red ribbons. And you said it in time, for you hoped, although you dared not breathe it, that its dress would be made by Miss Ada. You had not quite given up your belief in Santa, you stubbornly held on, but you had begun to guess that Santa might have a difficult time without Miss Ada's help. So, playing it safe, you wrote a letter and kneeling on the hearth in your mother's bedroom you watched for the moment when, if you let go, the up-draft from the flames would whoosh your message to the North Pole. But, having acquired a smidge of your mother's canniness, you also persuaded the Seventeen-year-old to take another letter out to Miss Ada's, in case Santa dropped by.

Poor Miss Ada, the town called her. After her old mother's death, she lived alone in the mosscovered house under tall cedars at the edge of the grave yard. The day before her wedding, Miss Ada's fiancé died of typhoid fever; and she was left on the edge of a wedding day she could not enter and could not leave. Sometimes, you'd see her in her white satin gown wandering among the tomb-

stones, stooping to stroke a carved lamb or rubbing the moss on an urn, and she'd be smiling and talking to herself, or maybe, laughing loud at something very funny. At other times she'd be sobbing. And you'd hide behind a cedar and listen, then everything would swing round inside you—and you ran home quick. When you got there you called, "Mama!" And when her calm voice answered, you said, "Nothing—just wanted to know where you were."

After a time, people noticed how thin she was, and slowly, they realized Miss Ada needed money for food. But nobody knew what to do. Until a poet in our town—who made up wonderful poems after he'd polished off half a pint or so which he kept by the rattan chair where he sat most days in his back yard under a chinaberry tree—suggested Miss Ada dress Santa's dolls. Everybody knew instantly this was exactly as it should be. And ever afterward, she dressed Santa's dolls and some for birthdays, too. And it was not long before little girls began to feel Santa hadn't treated them right if their dolls were not dressed by Miss Ada—although they didn't *know* it was Miss Ada, they

only half guessed it was; and the mystery, the doubt, rimming their faith gave ambience to the delicate garments.

The more the illuminated fountains gushed, the deeper the nine of us were plunged in financial complexities. For there were so many to buy presents for—not only each other but the grandmas and the cousins and the cook, and the cook's husband and her grandson and the nurse, and Desto and Japers and the washerwoman out at Mt. Pisgah, who came in once a week in her rickety wagon to bring the huge white bundles of washed and ironed clothes; and teacher at school and teacher at Sunday School.

To manage it all, we toted in wood, cleaned lamp chimneys, ran to the meat market for the steak for supper, swept Grandma's room, made our beds without being told, swept the tiled walks that led to the street, washed our mother's handkerchiefs, washed our father's socks, offered to wash his feet after he'd walked home from the office. And sometimes he'd let us, as he sat reading the

Savannah News or the *Florida Times-Union*. We'd bring a basin and mother's lavendar soap and wash his feet and powder them with the Spiro he liked to use, then slip a fresh pair of socks on the moist feet, and bring his carpet slippers. And sometimes, we'd hear him say to Mother, "The children are getting mighty thoughtful." And his blue eyes would twinkle and he'd chuckle and Mother's dark eyes would laugh and they seemed to have such nice secrets—though there were thunder and lightning times, too, and silences that raced your heart, but these you didn't think about at Christmas.

We evolved all kinds of money-making schemes, such as reselling our newspapers and magazines to the neighbors. But our mother stopped that one flat. One brother suggested we sell our summer clothes at a smash bargain in mill town, but Dad stopped that one. We settled for less speculative ventures, the older ones taking jobs in the stores after school hours. We kids earned what we spent. We were not rich people, not as wealth is thought of in the cities. We were just small-town people who lived in an ample and comfortable way. We were given little spending money: a nickel was nice, a dime was big, a quarter rich, a dollar was a dream.

The younger ones skittered along contenting themselves with whatever they could improvise for the grown folks. Once I gave my father a pincushion made of a piece of red velvet from an old hat of Mother's, which I scrunched up and filled with bird seed snitched from the shelf where the canary's food was kept, and centered with a gilt button found on the floor when my brother was home from military school. My father seemed to like it; he told me he'd never had a red velvet pincushion in all his life and had never used pins but he was not too old to learn, and he thought it was fine that I could do something besides rattle my tongue.

But the older ones didn't feel they could skin by like that. There was one historical year when the fifteen-year-old with his disciples, a thirteen-year-old brother, and the cook's grandson, named Town Marshal, decided we had neglected the parents. They should be given Nice Things—

things that could be heirlooms, Age Fifteen announced. He had been reading to Town and his brother novels about English manors and French châteaux, and lately he'd been specializing in Carlyle's *French Revolution*. Looking round our rambling barn of a house he couldn't find much the fourth and fifth generation would cling to—certainly nothing they'd lay down their lives for. He said to Age Thirteen and Town, "Take these old brass beds: do you know

what they are?" His empathetic audience shook their heads. "They're the status quo. Would you die for them?" No, the mob shouted. "O. K.," he said, "then we gotta do something." Age Thirteen and Town, like many disciples, increased in fervor more rapidly than did their mahatma and went round for days staring into space. Inclined to be absentminded, anyway, Age Thirteen became more so and left his violin—which as he said, was almost a Stradivarius— out on the back veranda in Big Granny's rocking chair.

This was about as absentminded as you can get. The only reason there was not total disaster was that Mother got there first. But Big Grandma seized the opportunity to say, "The boy is just like his grandfather, all time thinking about music and books, talking about things nobody can understand; the only reason you have to be thankful," she announced to her daughter, "is he can't speak six languages like his poor grandfather; if he starts that, he'll starve to death down here."

Little Miss Curiosity, a natural to head up any government's espionage system, caught on that something was brewing. She slipped away from Desto's granddaughter who was baby-sitting the younger ones, and hid behind the Cape jasmine bush.

Town was talking as usual—which was every moment Age Fifteen wasn't holding forth. The others were listening. Town was saying:

"Why don't we ketch the freight train when it slows down on Sandy Hill at Tuten's, and ride to New York?"

"Then what?"

"Then we could ketch a boat and hide in a corner somewheres and ride to that little French town named Have."

"Lee Have," corrected Age Thirteen.

"OK. Then we'd ketch another freight train to the castle—"

"What castle?"

"One we been studyin about—Verse All."

"Verse Alley," corrected Age Thirteen.

"Verse Illey," corrected Age Fifteen. "Then what," he pushed Town.

"Then we'd—we'd walk up those steps real slow and easy right into the Hall of Mirrors, like we had business there."

"What business?"

"Business with the king. I'm the ambassador from Africa and I have business with Louis the Fourteenth—and you two can be my retinue."

Silence.

Town glanced at Age Thirteen, "You can play your violin." Silence. "And you can play your guitar," glancing at Age Fifteen. Silence. Town, who was the soul of tact, studied the faces of his two friends. With a change of pace, he said, "I know what! I'll be the ambassador from Africa and you be the sheriff and deputy from Dixieland. How'd that be?"

"Fine," said his friends. Age Thirteen added slowly, "And we can wear a big silver star—"

Town interrupted. "The ambassador can wear one, too. All of us can wear a star," he added tactfully.

"You wear a crown," said Age Thirteen. "We wear a silver star."

"Nope," said Town firmly. "My name is Town Marshal and that gives me a right to wear a star. All of us can wear one."

"That makes sense," said Age Fifteen, who knew when he'd met his match. "Then what?" he asked Town.

"Then," said Town, "we get washed up for supper and eat a little somep'n and then we have a talk with the king; then the king says he's had a hard day, and he'd better get to bed and we say we tired, too. So—everything gets quiet and the help goes to bed and then we slip back into the Hall of Mirrors and while you two roll up a rug I take down a big gold looking glass and we sneak out the back door and make it for the freight train which is blowing down at the crossing and we know we better hurry, so we hot foot it down the road and the whistle is blowing two shorts so we know it's going to stop at the water tank and we—"

"Lord help us," said Age Fifteen, suddenly coming to. "Town, you the biggest fool in this family!"

"He is not," shouted Age Thirteen, "you the biggest fool in this family, you just scared to try it, me and Town we'd cut the king's head off to bring our parents some heirlooms—you all time thinking up things then when Town tells you how to do it, you get scared, that's what—you leave Town alone—"

"Kids!" sneered Age Fifteen and walked away.

But the next day he was holding forth. "Down to brass tacks," he was saying—a phrase of our father's. "Town, you quit your big talk, and you do, too," he said turning to Town's chum. "The two of you got work to do. We got to find some heirlooms. It's only eight days to Christmas. Now you go to the Supply Store and look over the place, go down in the basement and everywhere—there might be something; I'll go to the jewelry store and the hardware store—and the cotton warehouse—"

"And we'll go to the Opera House and look through that stuff—"

"Trash," said Age Fifteen. "Stage sets are trash, waste of time—"

"We going anyway," said Town. "Somep'n might turn up."

"Somep'n might," Age Thirteen.

Age Fifteen studied Town's face. "How you goin get there?"

The lights turned on from Town's chin to his hair line. "Easy," he said. "We goin slip round to the back of the Supply Store, then we walk like nothin on our minds to behind the hardware store, then we cut through to the livery stable and look round at the horses and when nobody's noticing we sneak in the back of the feed store, real easy, and go round the front way to Sandlin's mule lot and we stay there a little, then we stop at the calaboose and talk to everybody there and—"

"When you goin get to the Opera House?"

"We'll get there," said Town, still lit up. "We gotta

throw em off our tracks, see? We cut through the ball diamond and back round to Mr. Peeple's gin, then we head straight for the Opera House, but easy like we don't exactly know where we're going, then we stop by the grocery store and ask old Mr. Brown if there's somep'n we can do for him—"

"Better not," said Age Thirteen, "he'll find somep'n."

Town smiled in a superior way, "We don't *do* it, see?

we say yessuh but we don't *do* it, see? we just make like we're goin to then we light out for the alley fast as we can and when we come to the back of the Opera House, we shake the windows and find one we can push up and we climb in and then we go without making a sound up the back stairs—"

"I'll meet you at three-thirty, in front of the drug-store," said Fifteen.

"Thought you had a Christmas job," said Thirteen.

"I'll start day after tomorrow."

The next two afternoons were spent casing all the joints. Afterward, the three gathered at the boys' "garden house" to talk it over. (There was a g. h. for the girls and one on the opposite side of Mother's flower garden for the boys.) Miss Curiosity, whose extrasensory equipment was working overtime, slid through the woodhouse, round the back of Aunt Chloe's, backtracked, then crept round a clump of Cape jasmine and hid behind the boys' g. h. so she could find out what they were up to.

"Nothing fit to be an heirloom," Age Thirteen was saying.

"This town's full of trash," said Town.

"There's one watch that'd do," said Age Fifteen, "at the jewelry store; it has five diamonds, but it's a wrist watch and that's too new. You got to be careful about heirlooms, next year it might be out of style and nobody would look at it—" He studied Town's face. "What you think, Town?"

"Well, I tell you," said Town in a slow, judicious voice, "nothing in this town fit to be an heirloom cept one thing—and it's a beaut. It's a beaut and it won't go out of style—"

"Tell you, it won't do," urged Thirteen Year Old.

"Well now, I'm not so sure. It's a real beaut and it's not going to break up, it's built solid and the handles are made out of real silver—"

"You talking like Big Granma," said Fifteen, "get to

the point. What is it?"

Town glanced at Age Thirteen's rapt face. Age Thirteen shrugged in futile attempt to break the spell.

"Well," said Town, "It's the prettiest coffin you ever saw. We slipped up to the second floor when Mr. Pennington wasn't looking—"

"Went to see the appendix and the liver and egg they got there in alcohol," said the thirteen-year-old. "Town didn't get to see 'em." The others had when the WCTU lady lectured at school on the evils of drinking.

"We looked at that," said Town, "and then we looked at the coffins. And right in the front there was a beaut. It has big silver handles and silver knobs and it's gray and I opened it—"

"You—" Fifteen Year Old succumbed to total awe.

"Sure," said Town, "I just opened it to see what it looked like inside. Things these days, they're likely to look better outside than inside. It's a beaut, I'm telling you, all satin. I reached in and pulled at it—"

"You—" Fifteen was humbled to the dust.

"Sure. To see if it was strong. You gotta be careful these days. Everything seemed first class. It'll last easy to the fourth or fifth generation and I bet it looks even better then than—"

Fifteen Year Old couldn't speak. Horror and ecstatic admiration were tearing him to pieces. Town went on, "Nothing but trash in this town except—"

Fifteen was coming to. "Lord help us—" he whispered, "it's great—it's absolutely great—it's absolu—" then he caught a mean glimpse of reality. "Town, you're the craziest fool in this family, I swear to—"

"He is not," said Age Thirteen. "It makes sense. It won't wear out and it's a beaut, all right; real silver handles—"

"But how you goin use it?" Age Fifteen pushed. "Which one you goin to give it to?"

Silence. But only for a second. Town solved it. "Both," he said judiciously. "Give it to both. Then the one who needs it first will use it."

Town's powers of hypnosis were superb. All he needed do was relax and stare hard. He stared hard at Age Fifteen who muttered, "Fair enough."

But reality had the edge even on Town. "We can't do it," said the fifteen-year-old, after a long moment of hypnotic assent. He stopped. Studied the ground. Looked at Town, and once more the spell worked. "It'd be absolutely—it'd be absolu—" he lit out for the wild blue yonder— "You see, we let the kids go through their stockings first and play a minute or so with their little old dolls and little old toy stoves and teasets and little old red fire engine and all that, while the three of us sneak out to the woodhouse where we got it hidden then we bring it right through the hall and into—" He crashed. "Nope. We can't do it, Town. We just can't."

Town sighed. "Did cost a lot of money."

"How much?"

"Four hundard and fifty—"

Fifteen's eyes bugged out—

"You better not steal that coffin," yelped Miss Curiosity, "it's for old Mr. Askew sure as the world, he's dying and sure as the world it's for him—"

Paralysis set in. Town slowly lifted one finger, made the sign of the circle: that meant hold still. He said easy-like, "Well boys, reckon I'd better be helping my grandma and you better be helping yours—" and with that he got up real slow and made a dash round the g. h. and when Miss Curiosity saw him coming, she took to her heels through the lane, circled round the barn and back through the woodhouse into the rose garden—saw the three were gaining on her and there was nowhere to go but the magnolia tree, so she ran through the passageway of the house and pulled up the tree like a monkey and was half way to the top when the boys reached it. "You leave me alone," she shrieked, "Papa said everybody in this family had to treat each other like human beings."

"You ain't no human being," Town called up the tree where Miss Curiosity had now swung out to a high thin limb, that would not have held the big boys, and clung there swaying in the wind.

"You sho ain't," yelled Thirteen.

They stood peering up at her, utterly thwarted.

"Let's cut her liver 'n' lights out," suggested Town.

"We goin cut your liver 'n' lights out," yelled Thirteen.

And Miss Curiosity, sure as the world they would if

she came down, clung to that final sprout of the magnolia, until her father came home at supper time and promised her safe conduct to the dining room, under certain conditions.

Everybody went to work next day to earn Christmas

money and even Miss Curiosity heard no more talk of heirlooms.

Christmas Eve came. All day, Mother and Grandma and the cook and the two oldest sisters worked in the kitchen. Fruit cakes had been made for a month, wrapped in clean white towels and stored in the dark pantry. But the lean pork had to be ground for pork salad, the twenty-eight-pound turkey had to have its head chopped off, and then it must be picked and cleaned and hung high in the passageway between house and dining room, and then, of course, you had to put a turkey feather in your hair and make like you were Indians; then coconuts had to be grated for ambrosia and for the six-layered coconut cake and the eight coconut custard pies, and you helped punch out the eyes of the coconuts; then of course you needed to drink some of the coconut milk, and as you watched the grown-ups grate the nut meats into vast snowy mounds you nibbled at the pieces too small to be grated—and by that time, you felt sort of dizzy but here came the dray from the depot bringing the barrel of oysters in the shell (they were shipped from Apalachicola), and you watched them cover the barrel with ice, for you can't count on north Florida's winter staying winter. It was time, then, to lick the pan where the filling for the Lord Baltimore cake had been beaten and somebody laid down the caramel pan—but you tried to lick it and couldn't, you felt too glazy-eyed and poked out. And finally, you lay down on the back porch in the warm sun and fell asleep.

When you woke up it was almost dark. The sun had dropped behind the woodhouse. Curls of smoke floated from the chimney of the cook's house in the back yard. Her husband was smoking his pipe on the porch and Town, his grandson, was lounging on the steps reading a book.

Town read everything Thirteen and Fifteen read, although he went to school only three months each year, for that was all the school there was for Town to go to. But his two friends taught him what they learned each day and he kept right up with them—although, maybe, they didn't know they were teaching and he didn't know he was learning. They just liked to do everything together so they did it. Now Town's grandfather was speaking to him: you saw Town move inside to lie before the fire and continue his reading; you knew he had been told what your father told you, "It'll ruin your eyes in that light."

In the kitchen they were preparing supper. You didn't want it. You played round with your spoon. Your mother came to your chair, felt your cheek, leaned down and felt your head with her lips to see if you had fever. You liked this so much, sometimes you played sick to get her to do it. She decided you didn't need any Castoria (the family answer to everything wrong with children) but Big Granny called out to say she might as well give you Castor Oil, everybody ought to be given a jigger of Castor Oil on Christmas Eve to make way for Christmas.

Mother did not seem to hear but accelerated stocking-hanging. Twelve were hung. The foresighted had reserved Big Granny's weeks ahead, the laggards made do with Aunt Chloe's (first choice) or Mother's (second choice). The long black stockings hung from the mantel in Mother's bedroom each with a name on it.

Five o'clock, next morning, the little ones were scrambling round the fireplace, feeling in the dark for theirs.

Mother, in her bed, did not stir. Father, in the adjoining room, turned over, muttered *my my my*. The rule was, you tiptoed and you whispered and you looked through your stocking but you couldn't touch the big presents lying right there before you until you had dressed.

So you took down your knobby stocking and in the light from the fire which someone had thrown kindling on, you dug in. And all the time, there—on a fine new doll rocker—sat the beautiful doll Miss Ada (well, maybe) had

dressed but you dared not touch it until you had washed your face and put on your clothes. You stood and stared at it and then you saw a teaset and you stared at it and the suspense was almost unendurable. But at that moment, a big sister appeared and offered to help you dress quick, and then, suddenly, Mother was in her wrapper and our father was tiptoeing in from his room, making like he didn't know what it was all about. This big act of Absolute Astonishment which he staged each year gave an extra polish to an already shining moment. Where did it all come from! what a fire engine! what a doll! what a tea-set! what soldiers! what a rocking horse—

Finally, we went to breakfast. No verses on this day. We sat down to a table which held the same breakfast every Christmas: before my father's place, in an enormous platter, was a cold gelatiny hog's head which had been boiled with bay leaves and spices, a few pickled pig's feet were with it, and up and down the long table were three big platters of sausage and bowls of grits and plates of biscuits, and butter and syrup.

We waited for Mother. She came in from the kitchen, flushed from last-minute doings, and sat down. Then Fifteen and Thirteen got up again, looking solemn, walked to the corner of the bay window. With a fine flick of the wrist, the fifteen-year-old uncovered the small children's table (the overflow table when company was present). Behold! the future heirlooms. You felt a letdown, having overheard the plans and knowing what might have been there. But the others gaped admiration. The boys had presented the parents with eighteen plates, each with a splendid fish painted on it, and eighteen side dishes for the bones. The oldest then made a presentation speech on the necessity for heirlooms. He said in times of revolutionary unrest heirlooms had a most stabilizing effect, they gave a thrust to one's patriotism (or something to that effect), and he and his brother were making the gift not so much to the parents as to the fourth and fifth generation. And then everybody applauded, for he was a natural—you felt like applauding whenever you saw him.

(Later, you heard your father ask where in the name of heaven did the boys get enough money to buy all those dishes. They must have cost plenty! Mother said they probably did. "But where . . ." and then he did a double-take. "Not . . ." "I'm afraid so," was the reply. In January, when the bills came in, he found the donors had done what he half guessed and Mother's intuition confirmed: they had charged them to his account at the Supply Store.)

After the excitement of the unexpected gift subsided, our father took down the Bible and opened it at the second chapter of St. Luke. Nine pairs of eyes turned toward him as we waited to hear what we had heard every Christmas of our lives:

> *And it came to pass in those days that there went out a decree from Caesar Augustus, that all the world should be taxed. And Joseph also went . . . unto the city of David, which is called Bethlehem: . . . to be taxed with Mary his espoused wife, being great with child. And the days were accomplished that she should be delivered. And she brought forth her firstborn son, and wrapped him in swaddling clothes, and laid him in a manger. . . . And there were in the same country shepherds abiding in the field, keeping watch over their flock by night. And, lo, the angel of the Lord . . .*

As he read in his deep warm voice, we followed the words, knowing them by heart. We knew, too, that to him it was not only the story of the Christ Child but of Every Child, every new beginning, every new chance for peace on earth. When he was done, we bowed our heads: he thanked God for "all the good things which we do not merit" and asked His blessing on all who were suffering and in need in every country in the whole world, and then he asked for courage, courage to have vision, for "without vision the people perish."

The bay window was bright. Fire and cat were purring. Canary was at peace. Mother sat between her two eldest home from college, and her eyes were big and dark and somehow sad and tender, and there was flour on her nose. A good silence was settling on us. Then the youngest one said, "I fink Thesus was a fine little fellow"—and a sausage perched on top of the pile shivered and rolled off

the platter toward him. And everybody laughed and began to eat breakfast.

In the middle of the day we had dinner. But by the time the dinner bell rang and we assembled in the dining room, we had little space left for turkey and Mother's succulent dressing made of nuts and oysters and celery and eggs and bread and turkey "essence," for we had been nibbling all morning on raisins and candy and crystallized fruit and pecans (which were cracked and in bowls, everywhere). The next day, and the next, the results of the cooking and baking that had gone on for days would be more appreciated. After all, there is no better time to eat a piece of coconut pie than after you have been racing round for hours and someone says, Let's have a piece of coconut pie! You stop, everybody goes to the pantry, and you eat a piece of pie, then you get a spoon and scoop out a little cold turkey dressing, then you pick up an olive, then you take

a piece of stuffed celery left over from Christmas, and then you dash out to the back yard and climb up on the roof of the woodhouse and call the others to come up there . . .

On Christmas afternoon, we went visiting and our friends came visiting us and sometimes we'd meet half way between our houses. We girls had, of course, to show off our dolls and books and sewing baskets and manicure sets and the big boys had to show off their bicycles and shotguns and the little boys showed off their red wagons and fire engines. But before dark we were home again and a stillness settled down on the house.

And then, after things had been quiet a long time, our father would call out, "Where are the boys? It's about time to get our fireworks organized." But he knew: the boys—and the girls—were on their own beds, each in his own room or corner of a room, looking things over more closely or reading (books by the piles came at Christmas time). And now, each face had become its own, settling in its own

private curves, its own secret question marks, its own wisting or wondering lines. Each had crawled into his secret hide-out. Thirteen-year-old in his corner might be playing a new Mozart concerto he had wanted, or polishing his new gun; fifteen-year-old might be reading the new big dictionary which he had especially asked for; the nine-year-old philosopher might be squatting at the window, face like a buddha, looking deep into eternal matters as was his way. Suddenly one of them would stop, look

around as though he had never met the others and turn a
cartwheel or two, then they were all turning cartwheels
or wrasslin with each other and you'd hear them thumping
the floor and rolling off beds and maybe the slats would
fall out and the whole bed come tumbling down.

Then our father would call up and say, "I'm waiting,
boys!" And there'd be three or four *yessirs* and you'd hear
them dashing down the backstairs or the hall stairs and soon

you'd hear our father planning the fireworks which would
be set off at eight o'clock.

After the Big Illumination, when Roman candles and
rockets and cannon crackers were shot off on the front
lawn at the proper and dramatic moment by the big boys
and Town and our father, while the little ones raced round
with sparklers and firewheels and small firecrackers, all the
family and sometimes a few stray friends would dash into
the dining room for oyster stew, and oysters on the shell,

and fried oysters; and there'd be a waving of tomato cat-sup and horse-radish bottles and somebody would drop a raw oyster on a rug and a big sister would clean it up . . .

And now everything fades out. And one knows only that there must have been a slow stumbling exhaustion which ended in bed. And finally, the old house was still. And whatever was said was said by the toadfrog under-neath the house or by the great pillars which held the house and its children and the parents and Big Grandma or Little Grandma secure on their giant shoulders.

Every Christmas it was like this until the First World War. Then things turned upside down: the new world be-gan to squeeze the old too hard. The world market which the naval stores industry depended upon grew very dizzy indeed; we children of a small inland town heard daily talk of the seas and the ships, and the blockade, and the Germans and the Russians and the British and strange names and strange places entered our lives and have, of course, stayed there. I heard my father had "over-stretched" himself and I was sure he had; but I was as sure as could be that no matter how much "stretching" he had done he'd never fail to do what he set out to do, and the stretching would turn out to be his magic way of stepping across a wide chasm from where he was to a more exciting place.

But this time, it did not happen quite as I had expected. Our father lost his mills and his turpentine stills, the light plant and ice plant and store and the house that never quite ended—and we moved to our small summer cottage in the mountains.

There was nothing dismal about that moving, for my father departed like an explorer setting out for an unknown continent. He actually succeeded in convincing everybody but Mother that our new life was going to be more interesting than our old, that mountains were more beautiful than swamps and lily-covered ponds and oaks heavy with moss, that we'd never forget our first spring when we would see dogwood in bloom on the hills. (And of course, we have never forgot the beauty he spoke of—nor the deeper, mythic fascination of the swamps and cypress and sand and great oaks where we were born and where our memories still live.)

The move to the mountains, by the time Dad had planned it, had acquired all the drama and tension and highlights of a Great Hegira. He leased three big freight cars and stored the household furniture and the piano and the dishes and trunks full of Mother's linens and our things in two of them. (Certain large pieces of furniture they must have sold or given away, for I have never seen them since.) In the third freight car were the cow and the horses and the dogs and crates of pure-bred Leghorns from his farm plus feed for the long journey, plus farm implements plus tools and toys plus two of the brothers—and two of the young Negroes from the farm who were completely entranced by our father's stories of mountains and red earth and the great gorge at Tallulah Falls and asked to go along on this adventure.

It was a bit difficult to come down to the size of our small summer cottage after our father's big build-up but we managed it, somehow. He had a way of diverting us from nostalgic moods by arriving home from the little mountain town with two newly purchased feisty black mules, or a Duroc-Jersey sow, or maybe a hundred small apple trees. "What are we going to do with them?" Mother would ask quietly. "Mama, we are going to farm; this is going to be the finest little farm you ever saw. You will raise the prettiest pure-bred pigs in North Georgia and think what this hill will look like with a hundred apple trees in bloom in the spring!"

We were not alone in being poor. Times were hard in the South—much harder for most than for us, as our father often reminded us. Our region was deep in a depression long before the rest of the country felt it—indeed, it had never had real prosperity since the Civil War—only spotty surges of easy money. But even the bank did not know—and it knew plenty—how little money we managed on those years. It got worse instead of better as time passed. And there came a winter when my younger sister and I, who were in Baltimore preparing ourselves to be a great pianist (me) and a great actress (her) felt we were needed at home. We had been supporting ourselves in our schools but even so, we felt the parents needed us.

It was our barter year: Dad would take eggs to town, swap them for flour or cornmeal or coffee, and do it so casually that nobody suspected it was necessary. They thought he was so proud of his wife's Leghorns that he wanted to show their achievements to his friends at the stores. Eggs from the hens, three pigs which he had raised, milk and butter from the cow, beans he grew and dried, and apples from a few old trees already on the property—that was about it. It was enough. For Mother could take corn-meal, mix it with flour, add soda and buttermilk and melted butter, a dab of sugar and salt, and present us with the best hot cakes in the world. Her gravy made of drippings from fried side meat, with flour and milk added and crushed black pepper would have pleased Escoffier or any other

great cook. And when things got too dull, my sister and I would hitch up the two feisty mules to the wagon and go for as wild a ride as one wanted over rough clay winter roads.

Nevertheless, the two of us had agreed to skip Christmas. You don't always have to have Christmas, we kept saying to each other. Of course not, the other would answer.

We had forgot our father.

In that year of austerity, he invited the chain gang to have Christmas dinner with us. The prisoners were working the state roads, staying in two shabby red railroad cars on a siding. Our father visited them as he visited "all his neighbors." That night, after he returned from a three-hour visit with the men, we heard him tell Mother about it. She knew what was coming. "Bad place to be living," he said. "Terrible! Not fit for animals much less—" He sighed. "Well, there's more misery in the world than even I know; and a lot of it is unnecessary. That's the wrong part of it, it's unnecessary." He looked in his wife's dark eyes. She waited. "Mama," he said softly, "how about having them out here for Christmas. Wouldn't that be good?" A long silence. Then Mother quietly agreed. Dad walked to town —we had no car—to tell the foreman he would like to have the prisoners and guards come to Christmas dinner.

"All of them?" asked the chain-gang foreman.

"We couldn't hardly leave any of the boys out, could we?"

Close to noon on Christmas Day we saw them coming down the road: forty-eight men in stripes, with their guards. They came up the hill and headed for the house, a few laughing, talking, others grim and suspicious. All had come, white and Negro. We had helped Mother make two caramel cakes and twelve sweet potato pies and a wonderful backbone-and-rice dish (which Mother, born on the coast, called pilau); and there were hot rolls and Brunswick stew, and a washtub full of apples which our father had polished in front of the fire on Christmas Eve. It would be a splendid dinner, he told Mother who looked a bit wan, probably wondering what we would eat in January.

While we pulled out Mother's best china—piecing out with the famous heirloom fish plates—our father went from man to man shaking hands, and soon they were talking freely with him, and everybody was laughing at his funny —and sometimes on the rare side—stories. And then, there was a hush, and we in the kitchen heard Dad's voice lifted up: "And it came to pass in those days—"

Mother stayed with the oven. The two of us eased to the porch. Dad was standing there, reading from St. Luke. The day was warm and sunny and the forty-eight men and their guards were sitting on the grass. Two guards with guns in their hands leaned against trees. Eight of the men were lifers; six of them, in pairs, had their inside legs locked together; ten were killers (one had bashed in his grandma's head), two had robbed banks, three had stolen cars, one had burned down his neighbor's house and barn after an argument, one had raped a girl—all were listening to the old old words.

When my father closed the Bible, he gravely said he hoped their families were having a good Christmas, he hoped all was well "back home." Then he smiled and grew hearty. "Now boys," he said, "eat plenty and have a good time. We're proud to have you today. We would have been a little lonely if you hadn't come. Now let's have a Merry Christmas."

The men laughed. It began with the Negroes, who quickly caught the wonderful absurdity, it spread to the whites and finally all were laughing and muttering Merry

Christmas, half deriding, half meaning it, and my father laughed with them for he was never unaware of the absurd which he seemed deliberately, sometimes, to whistle into his life.

They were our guests, and our father moved among them with grace and ease. He was soon asking them about their families, telling them a little about his. One young man talked earnestly in a low voice. I heard my father say, "Son, that's mighty bad. We'll see if we can't do something about it." (Later he did.)

When Mother said she was ready, our father asked "Son," who was one of the killers, to go help "my wife, won't you, with the heavy things." And the young man said he'd be mighty glad to. The one in for raping and another for robbing a bank said they'd be pleased to help, too, and they went in. My sister and I followed, not feeling as casual as we hoped we looked. But when two guards moved toward the door my father peremptorily stopped them with, "The boys will be all right." And "the boys" were. They came back in a few minutes bearing great pots and pans to a serving table we had set up on the porch. My sister and I served the plates. The murderer and his two friends passed them to the men. Afterward, the rapist and two bank robbers and the arsonist said they'd be real pleased to wash up the dishes. But we told them nobody should wash dishes on Christmas—just have a good time.

That evening, after our guests had gone back to their quarters on the railroad siding, we sat by the fire. The parents looked tired. Dad went out for another hickory log to "keep us through the night," laid it in the deep fireplace, scratched the coals, sat down in his chair by the lamp. Mother said she had a letter from the eldest daughter in China—would Papa read it? It was full of cheer as such letters are likely to be. We sat quietly talking of her family, of their work with a religious organization, of China's persisting troubles after the 1911 revolution.

We were quiet after that. Just rested together. Dad glanced through a book or two that his sons had sent him. Then the old look of having something to say to his children settled on his face. He began slowly:

"We've been through some pretty hard times, lately, and I've been proud of my family. Some folks can take prosperity and can't take poverty; some can take being poor and lose their heads when money comes. I want my children to accept it all: the good and the bad, for that is what life is. It can't be wholly good; it won't be wholly bad." He looked at our mother, sitting there, tired but gently involved. "Those men, today—they've made mistakes. Sure. But I have too. Bigger ones maybe than theirs. And you will. You are not likely to commit a crime but you may become blind and refuse to see what you should look at, and that can be worse than a crime. Don't forget that. Never look down on a man. Never. If you can't look him straight in the eyes, then what's wrong is with you." He glanced at the letter from the eldest sister. "The world is changing fast. Folks get hurt and make terrible mistakes at such times. But the one I hope you won't make is to cling to my generation's sins. You'll have plenty of your own, remember. Changing things is mighty risky, but not changing things is worse—that is, if you can think of something better to change to. . . . Mama, believe I'll go to bed. You about ready?"

On the stairs he stopped. "But I don't mean, Sister, you got to get radical." He laughed. His voice dropped to the soft tones he used with his younger children. "We had a good Christmas, didn't we?" He followed our mother up the stairs.

My younger sister and I looked in the fire. What our future would be, we did not know. The curve was too sharp, just here; and sometimes, the dreaming about a curve you can't see round is not a thing you want to talk about. After a long staring in the fire, we succumbed to a little do-you-remember. And soon we were laughing about the fifteen-year-old and Town and the thirteen-year-old and their heirloom year, and the hog killing and the Song of Solomon and the tree-shaking and Big Grandma's sausage, the best as our mother used to say that anybody could make, with just enough red pepper and sage . . .

And now the fire in front of us was blurring.

My sister said softly, "It was a large Christmas."

"Which one?"

"All of them," she whispered.

R * R * R * R * R * R * R * R * R * R

Christmas Kitchen
Fifty Years Ago

R * R * R * R * R * R * R * R * R * R

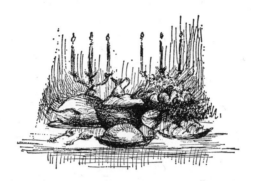

Our old kitchen returns in my memory, decked out in its winter ways. Always as I think about it a fire is burning easy and slow in the fireplace, and one of the cats is sleeping at its edge, and somebody, Big Grandma or Mother or the cook, is rocking in the chair near the cat with a pan on her lap preparing something for dinner or supper.

The kitchen was a big wide room on the southwest side of the house, full of yellow light in the afternoon; and this yellow light always smelled like spice cake, or spareribs slowly browning, or maybe sweet potato pies at the crusty moment of being considered "done" and ready to set out on a long deal table to cool.

In the big black iron stove there was a murmur of wood burning in slow steady combustion, just right for the

pies. A woodbox was at the side of the stove stacked with
various kinds of wood: resinous kindling for a sudden
flame, splintered dry pine for a quick breakfast fire, a
little green pine to temper the dry pine, oak split into the
proper size and length for the long haul of the four-hour
roasting which a fresh ham requires.

Mother and the cook were expert with a wood stove
and knew just how to encourage or dampen its ardor by
their skilled mixing of kindling and pine and oak and their
knowing twist of the damper on the stove pipe, and their
subliminal awareness that the time had arrived to shift a
pan or kettle from one side of the stove to the other.

I can see my mother now opening the wide oven,
putting her hand in to test its temperature, just as she put
her lips to our foreheads to see if we had fever. Her sense of
warmth was as accurate as any thermometer. I never heard
her blame the temperature of the oven for her rare failures

with cake. She would lift a layer, weigh it delicately in her hands, and say the cake was "sad" because she had put a little too much sugar in it, or heavy because she had added a smidge too much flour.

We children adored sad cakes; for we could eat at once the fallen stuff, delicious in its extra sweetness and crunchiness. (Mother would not have let it enter her dining room, it would have shamed her too much.)

Beyond the big stove was the kitchen sink. For years there was no actual sink but a long table covered with zinc on which were two or three big dishpans. Dishes were washed in pan Number 1, rinsed in pan Number 2; the pots were soaked in pan Number 3. An orderly procedure. Somebody toted in water from the artesian well in the back yard, and I am sure all nine of us did our share but since I was one of the younger children, this part of it fades out. By the time I was eight, we had "running water," as we called it, in the kitchen, and a real sink, and several bathrooms. But my mother or the cook—perhaps both—was reluctant to give up the old ways entirely, for I remember with eyes more mature than an eight-year-old's that dishwater was carried to the back yard to be poured around certain plants which our mother thought profited from the fine mixture of grease and "richness."

Extending from the far end of the kitchen was a porch latticed in (and later screened) where the screened safes were kept for cooked food and a monstrous-sized icebox our father had had built at his mills. It was made of heavy oak timber, some of it four inches thick; and the whole affair was lined with zinc. To lift its lid was impossible without pulley and chain. I suspect our mother lived in constant fear of a decapitated child. Perhaps that is why only the raw meats and fish and other unappetizing foodstuffs were kept there with the ice.

The milk from our Jersey cow (she gave four gallons a day) was always kept in a special milk-safe screened with cheesecloth (before metal screens were available); and this safe was presided over by my mother, who was not certain where typhoid germs came from but had a canny notion that dirty milk could precipitate a dozen mean ills in addition to the dramatic one of typhoid.

How delicately she skimmed those pans of milk! They were large round shallow pans, chosen because cream can be skimmed more easily from shallow pans. I would stand beside her, sunk deep in a sweet orgy of sensuous delight, as I watched her fold heavy yellow cream back from the pale blue milk beneath, then skillfully swoop the thick roll up with her big spoon into the cream bowl. I'd whisper, "Oh Mama, let's have some hot gingerbread for supper all covered with cream," and she'd look at me and say "Sssh . . ." as though the cream were a sleeping baby. She handled it as gently as if it were one, just as she handled tender plants when setting them out in the beds she had made for them. But though she said *sssh*, nearly always the hot gingerbread would appear at supper covered with the clotted cream as a special treat for the nine of us.

By the milk-safe, in the corner, was kept the churn where butter was made. Every other day, the grandmothers churned. The earthenware tall churn would be washed with hot water and soap, carefully dried, put by the fireplace near the rocker. The heavy cream was poured in it and quarts of "clabber" (sour milk that had thickened to a delicate firm jelly-like consistency in the unrefrigerated temperature). One of the grandmothers would settle in the rocker and begin her task. *Flop . . . flop . . . flop . . .* the churning made this sound to me as I'd squat there watching. Finally, under the repetitive up-and-down motion, lumps of butter formed and the clabber turned to delicious buttermilk. This chemistry fascinated me. I would beg to understand exactly how it happened. Mother or Dad would talk about emulsion, about fat cells, etc. But this reasonable explanation could not get into my imagination, where the strange wonderful transformation of cream into butter had crawled up beside ghosts and angels and fairies and become an act almost as magic as spinning gold out of straw.

Finally, Big Grandmother gathered the butter into a dish and then beat it and pressed it and beat it and pressed until every drop of milk had been separated from the yellow glistening butter. Then the wooden mold was brought out, the butter packed into it, left there a moment, then eased on to a tray in a half-pound round stamped with a sheaf of wheat on top. When all the half-pounds had been molded, this creation was covered with a snowy white piece of an old tablecloth, or worn-out napkin and laid away in the milk-safe.

In this cavernous, bright, spice-laden kitchen the Christmas preparations began in late November, for the fruit cakes were always made early and set aside in the dark pantry to season.

I don't see how my mother could have managed without the big enameled dishpans at such a time. She'd sit at the wide table alongside Big Granny or Little Granny and the cook cutting orange peel and raisins, citron and ginger and pecans, until one of the pans would be filled with the sticky spicy mess. Then she would measure into another pan flour by the quart and sugar by the pint. She'd leave

this, go to the pantry, come back with a basket filled with six or seven dozen eggs. I liked the creamy-brown ones best and would ask to be permitted to count out the two dozen needed. Then Mother would break them, giving each a sharp nip on the edge of the table and depositing its undisturbed contents, freed of the shell, into the pan. The whole affair was elegant: golden orbs of eggs floating in islands of white . . . Mother's quick, dexterous movements as she went about her work . . . everything calmly moving toward the creation she was intent on. She was an artist in her own kitchen and there was a deep pleasure in her eyes as she gently pushed prying little ones away, and went on with her creating.

The day came when I must have my try at breaking an egg—which, somewhere in me, had become almost as ta-

boo as setting fire to the house or flinging one of her Haviland china plates to the floor. But now I was seven and grown up enough to try and she gave her permission. I stood trembling for five minutes on the edge of that precipice before I could take the fatal step. But I took it. I cracked the egg. Then hesitating again, I brought on disaster by spilling the egg on the floor. But Mother did not scold: she said, It happens; let's clean it up. We cleaned it up. Then she said, Try again. And I tried again and did it. And I am not sure any triumph in my life ever pleased me more than that successful act.

Now, over the fruit and nuts, were sprinkled cinnamon and nutmeg and mace and a little grated lemon peel. The nuts and fruit and flour and sugar and eggs were finally mixed well together in the biggest pan of all. Someone had greased the four-inch-deep cake pans and lined them with brown paper and now they were filled and placed in shallow biscuit tins lined with a half-inch of water for the slow steam-baking they required.

But for me, the making of fruit cake never quite reached the mouth-watering excitement of watching our mother do her famous turkey dressing. To experience this involved your glands, senses, mind, heart and soul.

It took place on Christmas morning. And no matter how absorbed I might be with new dolls and new books I'd be on hand to witness this great spectacle:

First, she crushed the contents of a dozen or more boxes of Uneeda Biscuits in a deep bowl. On these crushed crackers she then poured the "essence" which had resulted from browning and simmering for two hours the neck, liver, gizzard and wing tips of the twenty-eight-pound turkey. If the essence did not dampen the crackers sufficiently—and it never did—she then "stole," as she said, three or four cups of the most delicious-smelling stock from the turkey roasting pan and added to the mixture. This stealing always sent me into giggles but I'd keep glancing up at her face to be sure she was joking, for unlike my father she joked rarely and when she did, she joked so drily that we were never quite sure she meant it as a joke. Anyway, after the theft of the turkey stock, she put in the dressing six or seven cups of finely chopped celery, a few celery seeds, salt, pepper, a little chipped onion (not much) a half-pound of homemade butter (depending on the richness of the essence) and two dozen eggs. This was well stirred, then two quarts of pecans were added, and two quarts of oysters and a cupful or so of oyster liquor. The whole thing was now stirred for five minutes or more, tasted, a little sage added, a mite more pepper, and then after staring hard at it, Mother would go to the stove, pick up the kettle and pour a bit of steaming water into the pan to soften it a little more. This was IT. Mother then pushed some of it into the turkey pan—not much, for the turkey was cooking and already had a sausage stuffing in it. Then, after looking at it again for a long moment, and tasting it once more, she poured this delicious mess into deep baking dishes and set it aside to be cooked for thirty or forty minutes shortly before dinner. When served, it would be firm but fluffy, with just enough crispy bits of pecans and succulent oysters.

By this time, the big sisters had filled silver dishes with candies and nuts and stuffed dates, and glass dishes were filled with homemade pickles and olives; somebody was stuffing the celery with cheese and someone else was easing the jellied cranberry sauce into one of Mother's fancy flutey porcelain dishes. The cook, or perhaps Big Grandma, had prepared the sweet potatoes for candying and they were now on the back of the stove gently simmering in water, sugar, butter, orange peel and cinnamon. The rice

would be cooked during the last twenty-two minutes before the dinner bell was rung, but already the gravy had
been made and thickened with chipped-up liver, gizzard,
and hard-boiled eggs.

The pork salad and Waldorf salad, made early, were
kept in the ice-cold pantry until just before dinner when
they were placed on the sideboard in two hand-painted
bowls. Also on the sideboard were fruit cake, caramel cake,
six-layered coconut cake, Lord Baltimore cake, lemon-
cheese cake, and several coconut pies. Our father always
ate a slice of coconut pie but the rest of us preferred the
traditional ambrosia for Christmas dessert, with a sampling
of all the cakes.

Since the Greeks there have been ambrosias and ambrosias. Ours was fit for the most exacting Olympian taste,
for it was of a special delicacy since the oranges were not
sliced but each plug of fruit lifted out of its inner skin
and kept as nearly whole as possible. A layer of these frag-
ile orange plugs would be put in the bowl, then a layer of
finely grated fresh coconut (not shredded), then a sprinkling of sugar, then another layer of orange, coconut, and
so on until the bowl was full. It might have tasted better
served to you as you reclined on a floating cloud but I doubt
it.

And now, the dinner bell rang and in we ran, already
too stuffed by our nibblings since five A.M. to do more than
admire, sniff, and taste here and there. But no matter how
poked-out I was I made a miracle somehow and pushed in

two helpings of turkey dressing. The other things could wait until tomorrow or the next day or the next.

All of this was unforgettable, seeping not only into memory but into bones and glands.

But even Christmas Week did not delight the palate more than did hog-killing week. I still am not sure whether turkey dressing, even my mother's, won a clear victory over liver-'n'-lights stew. The stew was cooked two days on the back of the stove, spiced with onions, black pepper and salt and a clove or two, and seasoned with bits of fatty-lean pork.

First, the liver and the lights (lungs) and sweetbreads

of a hog were cut into small pieces and browned with the
bits of fatty-lean pork, in an enormous black iron kettle.
Water was then added, and the kettle pushed back on the
stove where it could cook slowly, after the onions and
black pepper and salt were added. At the end of two days
of slow simmering, this delicacy was ready to eat. We
liked it best with hot fluffy cornbread or with grits. I have
often wondered why we cannot have it, today. Is it necessary to kill one's own hogs in order to enjoy what is surely
one of the most delicious of provincial dishes?

Of course, along with the liver-'n'-lights stew came
the fresh-made sausage (with just the right amount of sage
and red pepper and fat) for breakfast; and roasted spareribs, a few nights later, for supper. And the following week
we were likely to have backbone and rice for dinner.

And now suddenly, because it is winter in the memory,
one smells oysters roasting in the shells. This roast took
place in the back yard on a circular sheet-iron saw which
our father had sent from the mill, and under which a fire
was made. The greedy memory of childhood holds it all:
oysters and turkey dressing and liver-'n'-lights and pork
salad and pecans and ambrosia: food that enhanced childhood Christmases and becomes now a mouth-watering
memory that returns each winter of one's life, however
far away the old kitchen may be.

For our family, it is gone forever. We are left only
with its smells and sounds and tastes, and a few "receipts"
of the family's traditional dishes.

Some of these I shall write down here. Remember,
they are not accurately measured and weighed. Our kitchen
was no laboratory, it was a gourmet's studio where the art-

ist played the major role; an artist whose hand was so sensi-
tized to quantity and weight and the eye to appearances
that scales and cups were often laid aside—except for the
making of cakes. But all real cooks know about pinches
and smidges, and a fluff of this, a dusting of that, so perhaps these old receipts will not be a puzzlement to them.

The Famous Turkey Dressing

We made it in my childhood with Uneeda Biscuits,
but I find unsalted crisp plain crackers of any brand as
good.

For six people, four cups of crushed crackers should
be sufficient. Boil neck, liver, gizzard (after browning in a
little butter) for at least two hours or until tender; add water now and then, if necessary. You should have two cups
of strong stock, seasoned with salt and pepper and two
stalks of celery. Remove the celery and add stock to the
crackers. Then add two cups of diced fresh celery; one cup
of nuts, one cup of oysters. A half-cup of oyster liquor will
improve this mixture. Chip a small amount of onion—no
more than half a teaspoonful—add a skimpy bit of garlic
(if you like) but no more than a bare suggestion (one half
a small bud, chipped). Add a pinch of thyme, a pinch of
sage. I usually add a few sliced ripe olives and a few mush-
rooms, which I think enhance the flavor. Now, as did my
mother, "steal" a little rich stock out of the turkey pan—
as much as you can spare, taking care that you leave plenty
for gravy. Add three eggs and stir several minutes. You
should now have a soft, not soupy, mixture. If you do

not, add a bit of hot water. Or if too soupy, add a slice of broken-up bread, or a few more crackers. Now put in as much butter as your family's health can take. A large tablespoon is plenty for my modern taste. It should melt in the warm mixture as you stir.

The dressing is ready now for your casseroles and should fill two small ones or one large one. Let it stand an hour, then cook 30 minutes; keep warm for dinner.

Coconut Custard Pie

There are recipes for coconut custard pie easily available. The point is: use *freshly grated coconut* and plenty of it, and add it to a standard baked-custard mixture. I use 4 eggs well beaten and 2 cups of milk, with 5 scant tablespoonsful of sugar, 1 teaspoonful of butter and a pinch of salt. Dust this with nutmeg. Make a flaky pie pastry, line a medium pie pan, pour in the mixture, after stirring into it a cup and a half of coconut. Start it off in the oven at 400 degrees, to brown the crust a little, let it cook for six or seven minutes at this heat, then lower the heat to 325 or 300. Custard separates if cooked too rapidly. Cook until a knife blade can be slipped in the custard and come out clean. Should serve six people. We serve it with a dab of whipped cream.

Christmas Ambrosia

Ambrosia is made of tender oranges and freshly grated coconut, sprinkled with enough sugar to make it delicately sweet. Peel oranges, use sharp knife to get off most of the skin of the fruit, then slip the plugs of fruit out whole when you can. A layer of orange, a layer of grated coconut, a sprinkling of sugar, then another layer, still another until your bowl is full. It improves when allowed to set for a few hours, or even overnight, in a cool place.

Six-layered Coconut Cake

Use any good recipe for a light, smooth silver cake— that is, a cake with five or six egg whites in it and no yellows—of a quantity that will make six very thin layers. You have already grated two large coconuts. When your six thin layers of cake are done and you have set them on a rack to cool, you put two cups of sugar in a small boiler, and a cup of water and a tablespoonful of Karo syrup, and a lump of butter. When this makes a soft ball, it is ready. You let it cool a little so you can handle it. Then you put some of it (or all if you need it) into a bowl and put two-thirds of your coconut in. If you have too much syrup, don't use it all; hold back, but use two-thirds of the coconut. You spread this filling—it is mainly coconut held together by the syrup—between layers as you stack them up. Now after the top has had its spread of this coconut concoction, you are ready to ice your cake. You make a standard white icing: sugar, water, a little Karo syrup and cream of tartar (if you wish) cooked until it spins and crackles. You have in the meantime whipped up the whites of two eggs. Now, slowly pour your syrup into the whipped-up egg whites as you beat. Continue to beat until it thickens and does not run when you try it in a saucer. Then ice the entire surface of the cake with this. Immediately, the rest of the coconut should be patted gently into the icing on top and sides. Keep adding coconut until it will take no more. You have here, of course, the best cake in the world—and I am not forgetting the chocolate torte of Vienna.

Sweet Potato Pone, Fancied Up

This is not for Christmas but it is a hearty winter dessert to try now and then.

You grate the raw sweet potatoes. Since size and texture of sweet potatoes differ, it is hard for me to give you here the proper measurements. Let's try three cups of grated raw sweet potato; add to this three cups of milk, and three well-beaten eggs. Put in a dusting of nutmeg. Add a cup of pale brown sugar. (Taste: do not have too sweet.) Pour into a baking pan. (It should be about an inch and a half thick.) Cook slowly in the oven, much as you would bake a sweet potato. Begin it at a heat of 400, turn to 325 for the rest of the time. An hour should be about right. Serve this with clotted cream—if you have such— or with whipped cream. Add pecans if desired.

Pork Salad

I doubt that many people would dare eat it in this day of cholesterol doubts, etc., but it was powerful good, and it never made one of the little Smiths ill. First, you baked a fresh pork ham. And, perhaps, had one meal from it. You then cut the lean meat into small pieces (about 3 cups for six or eight people). You diced a cupful of celery, a cupful of apple, and added this to the mixture. You also added pecans cut small. You seasoned this with a homemade cooked salad dressing which had plenty of vinegar in it. This is it; and it is good. Especially when served with pickled peaches.